Walla Wa
County Librarie

How to Tie Your Shoes

Xóchitl Justice Press, San Francisco, CA

Library of Congress Control Number: 2014946104

ISBN: 978-1-942001-02-7

Second Edition March 2015

10 9 8 7 6 5 4 3 2 1

WORDS MATTER

How to Tie Your Shoes

Joshua Johnson
Edited by Margaret Richardson

Xóchitl Justice Press
San Francisco, CA

This is a guide to learn how to tie your shoes.

Remember these directions
like a poem or a song.

1st

The first step is to put on your socks and shoes.

2nd

Second, crisscross your laces.

3rd

Third, bring one lace under the other,
and pull both laces to tighten them.

4th

Fourth, make two loops,
like bunny ears.

5th

Fifth, push one lace under the other, and pull tight to make a knot.

Sixth, if you will be jumping,
running, or playing sports,

GOLDEN STATE
WARRIORS
GOLDEN STATE
30

6th

double knot the two loops.

Now you know all of the
steps to tie you shoes.

NO EXCUSES!

Ordinal Numbers

Ordinal numbers can help you follow directions.

English	Numeral + Suffix	Spanish
fir**st**	1 + **st** = 1st	primero
seco**nd**	2 + **nd** = 2nd	segundo
thi**rd**	3 + **rd** = 3rd	tercero
four**th**	4 + **th** = 4th	cuarto
fif**th**	5 + **th** = 5th	quinto
six**th**	6 + **th** = 6th	sexto

A Xochitl Justice Press/ Prince Hall Partnership

Xochitl Justice Press is a nonprofit organization focusing on community partnerships, research, teaching, and publishing.

Prince Hall Computer Learning Center began as a grassroots project to provide tools and activities to empower youth from the Western Addition community of San Francisco.

This book was published with generous support from the Jesuit Foundation.

AUTHOR

Joshua Johnson is in 8th grade. He wanted to write this book to help children learn how to tie their shoes because it was hard for him when he was little.

EDITOR

Margaret Richardson is a Master's/ Credential candidate in the School of Education at the University of San Francisco.

EDWIN M. LEE, MAYOR
PARTNERSHIPS & ENGAGEMENT

Xóchitl Justice Press

CPSIA information can be obtained
at www.ICGtesting.com
Printed in the USA
LVIC04n2157150915
454362LV00006B/16